Everything 'round Us Is Praise

To Carol —
Our lives are
based on seasons
may most if not all
of your seasons lead
you to praise God.

Peace ~
Diane.

Joy Cowley

Everything 'round Us Is Praise

Extraordinary Prayers for Ordinary Days

Photography by Terry Coles

AVE MARIA PRESS Notre Dame, Indiana 46556

Joy Cowley is the author of several novels and hundreds of children's books. Terry Coles, who created the photographs in *Everything 'round Us Is Praise*, is Joy's husband. They live on the south island of New Zealand.

© 1997 by Ave Maria Press, Inc.

International Standard Book Number: 0-87793- 628-5
Book design and cover photograph by Katherine Robinson Coleman.
Printed and bound in the United States of America.

Library of Congress Cataloging-in-Publication Data
Cowley, Joy.
Everything 'round us is praise : extraordinary prayers for ordinary days
/ Joy Cowley ; photographs by Terry Coles.
   p.   cm.
   ISBN 0-87793-628-5
   1. Prayers. I. Title.
BV245.C69   1997
242'.8—dc21
               97-13917
               CIP

Contents

Introduction

On our family bulletin board in the hall, pinned amidst photos, postcards, and price lists from the Chinese take-outs, there's a special poem entitled "Family Hymn," taken from *Everything 'round Us Is Praise.* The postcards come and go, and there's a new price list for the take-outs every other month, but the psalm has stayed there, enjoying pride of place for nearly a year now.

It's pure magic for tired parents trying to see salvation history being worked out in the chaotic lives of three small children. We dash past it to change diapers; we lean beside it as tricycles careen past; we face it head-on coming out of the kids' bedroom when the last light is finally extinguished.

The psalm points to the presence of God in the tireless, wonder-filled, irrepressible world of children. I have read it so many times beneath drooping eyelids, most often when I want to see spelled out what I feel but can't put into words. My spirit soars on the last line as it cuts to the heart of the matter and promises that there is in all this a "shortcut to holiness."

St. Paul said it simply: That is the mystery, Christ among people. And in every age, writers have been trying to put their finger on that mystery, trying to pin it down, trying to see the elusive movements of God in our lives and the ordinary circumstances of living. Joy Cowley is in that tradition that reaches back to and beyond the psalmists of the Old Testament.

It's not an easy task. The vision is not a long, clear one. The sky is full of clouds and the Holy Spirit moves ever so silently in the hearts of believers.

We suffer most from a lack of that vision when all we see are dark clouds hanging low and not what lies beyond them. In *Everything 'round Us Is Praise,* Joy Cowley and photographer Terry Coles are constantly pointing beyond, aware of a "big, bright, beautiful God" (Joy's phrase), who holds it all together. Their truest instincts are delight and wonder as they raise our sights to the God beyond and the life of God within.

Both Joy Cowley and Terry Coles have the gift of capturing a world that is alive to the senses. Their insights are anchored in a flesh-and-blood world. There is not spiritual escapism; the hand of God is there in the midst of creation.

On re-reading these psalms, I realize that the collo-
quial language is a great deliverance. It delivers us
from that beguiling but false notion that God is best
described in theological language and is most at
home behind stained glass windows. The everyday,
twentieth-century language of these psalms speaks
more insightfully of the real God who lives and
moves in the real world, a God who penetrates our
humdrum existence and shares our suffering.

These psalms belong together, published in one vol-
ume. Taken together, they leave one with the strong
sense of a writer with her feet on the ground, firmly
planted in the soil, but reaching, reaching.

~Michael Fitzsimons

Morning Hymn

Good morning, my Friend God.
I give you the voyage of this day,
that to be, which is already yours,
adding to it my rejoicing,
a shout of praise. Amen. Amen.
You are the wind: fill up my sails.
You are the water: run fast beneath my keel.
And I will sing in the wind
and dance over the water,
God, my Friend, oh God, my Friend.
You are the light: enfold me.
You are the darkness: embrace me.
You are pain: hollow me.
You are love: overflow me.
The storms of change are you,
and the peace of tranquil waters.
You are all these things, Friend God,
and I thank you. Amen. Amen.
May I journey without fear
through all your seasons.

In emptiness let me find fullness.
In imprisonment let me find freedom.
Render me passive in your will
and I shall be most active,
moving with you in everything,
seeing you in everything,
knowing you in everything.
Amen. Amen.

*C*hild's Play

Father Mother God,
every now and then you call me
to drop my burdens at the side of the road
and play games with you.
I respond sluggishly.
Carrying burdens can make me feel important
and sometimes I'm afraid to drop them
in case I suddenly become invisible.
But when I do let go for a while,
how simple life seems—
and how beautiful.

God of play and playfulness,
thank you for castles in the sand,
for swings and slides and soap bubbles,
kaleidoscopes, rainbows,
and wind to fly kites.
Thank you for child-vision
of flowers and stones and water drops,
for child-listening to the universe
humming inside a seashell.
Thank you for showing me once again,
a creation filled with laughter
and the enjoyment of your presence.
And thank you, thank you,
dear Mother Father God,
for the knowledge
of your enjoyment of me.

$\mathcal{S}$hells

This morning we walked along a beach
which seemed to be full of God's presence.
Sky, sea, sand, they were all alight,
splash and dazzle, sparkle, shimmer,
dancing in a celebration of love.

Everything 'round us was praise.

Then we came to a bed of shells.
They were lying halfway between the tides,
as neat as a parable.

Some of the shells were turned up
like cupped hands filled with gift.
All that was beautiful in the day
was contained in their openness.
But others were turned face down
with their backs to the celebration,
enclosing nothing but their own darkness
and emptiness.

Light. Dark. Full. Empty.
Open. Closed. Yes. No.
It gave us something to think about
as we continued along the beach.

Growth

If a tree were capable of reflection
would it have doubts about its growth?
Would it worry endlessly
about the direction it should take,
or when it should produce new leaves?
Would it sometimes imagine
that its life was without design?
Would it think that its height and shape
had been self-determined
through random acts of will
amounting more to good luck
than good management?

Because that's what I'm like.
True, I feel God working in my life,
but at no given time
is the direction clear to me.
I seem to have so many decisions
to make about the future
that I'm always concerned
about choosing the wrong thing.

But then, just as I imagine
that I'm acting out of confusion,
I stop and look back
on my journey until now.

What do I see?

From my birth to the present time
there is a clear straight path.
Everything I thought was deviation,
everything I counted as unnecessary,
missed, wasted, wrong, foolish,
is part of that straight path.
I see that an infinitely loving God
has used every thread of my life
to weave a perfect fabric of truth.
Don't ask me how.

In awe, I surrender my confusion,
knowing only these two things:
that as long as I choose to grow,
my loving God will take care
of the other choices in my life;
and that as a tree must grow towards light,
so must I grow towards God.

Language

I know that God exists beyond words
but all the same, I believe
that words can take us a long way
to the discovery of God in our lives.
Language can bring us unexpectedly
to the edge of God-awareness.
Parable, mantra, canticle, or chant,
the fresh naming of things by children,
words of love from a friend,
they can all turn locks in our hearts
so that the unnamable Presence,
the Word beyond all words,
can pour itself into our lives.

I also know that generally,
the language we use describes
our system of values on this earth,
and the things we say about God
come out of our own experience
of those values.

I ask my loving Creator
for the grace to use words wisely.
May I not try to own or contain God
in language limited to suit me.
May I not try to make God small,
in my own image.
May I not divide God and God's world
according to human ideas.

And may I keep the full shining meaning
of those words which really do
open me to God's presence,
words like Eucharist and Mystery,
Transcendence and Love
and Christ Jesus.

Hands

This morning, Lord,
these hands planted lettuce,
fed chickens, children, cat, sparrows,
and skimmed seeds off a batch of plum jam.

This morning, like any other day,
there were beds to make, washing to be done,
and a patch sewn on the knee of a child's jeans.

This afternoon, Lord,
one of these hands got a blister from the ax handle
and the other, a splinter from kindling wood,
but the afternoon brought deeper pain
when my hands closed tight to hide anxiety
then later opened to brush away tears
before anyone could notice.
It's been a day of ups and downs
with not much quiet in between.

Now, this evening, Lord,
I come forward to receive you
and hold out these hands like a cup
for the bread of your sacred body.

And I discover
that as you bless my hands with your presence,
so do you bless all their efforts.
All the planting, baking, cleaning, mending,
everything touched, everything tended,
all my fears and tears, my loving, my hurting,
the whole-up-and-down day, Lord,
is suddenly Eucharist.

Old Wood

There is something inside us
which wants to pay homage to things spent,
whether they be bones of animals or trees,
old ruins, or even last year's calendar.
To touch a relic of the past
is to feel the chain of life unbroken,
what was flowing into *what is* and *what will be*
in a continuous movement, forward and up.

I know that I am in error
if I ignore the present
in my dream for the future,
or if I try to reverse the flow
and live for yesterday.
And yet, I am this strange mixture
of hope and nostalgia,
investing in time unborn,
clinging to days that are dead,
often missing out on what is.

Dear Lord, give me the grace
to hold the past lightly
and to lay no claim to the future.
May my reverence for old wood
and my eagerness for new seasons,
enrich this present time of growth
and find their rightful place
in the greenness of now.

*A*nswers

Dear Friend,
I remember the time
when I thought I had all the answers.
I was so sure of my knowledge about you.
I read books of great teachings,
listened to fine sermons,
exchanged views of Scripture,
discussed, argued, scorched others
with my enthusiasm.

How necessary it was
to pour all experience of you
into a tight container of words!

All the time, dear Friend,
you smiled and led me on,
over the walls of imagery,
through fences of ideas,
gently showing me that walls and fences
have a rightful place in journey,
that they are there for support and shelter
and that when it's time to move on,
they will be no obstacle to progress.

I am still addicted to words
and I still need to hold you
in ideas and images,
though loosely now, in an open web.
But no longer do I have any answers.
You, dear Friend,
have taken away the questions.

$\mathcal{D}$o Dogs Go to Heaven?

As a small child, I anguished over the question:
"Do dogs go to heaven when they die?"
People told me they didn't, but one day
I met a woman who lived very close to heaven
and just as close to earth, and she said:
"Now, my dear, just you listen to me.
God made everything in this world
out of his love. And I mean everything.
Flies, ducks, mosquitoes, fish, cats, and dogs.

Every single creature's got a pinch of God in it,
and like you've always been told,
there's just no way God can die.
When a creature's life runs out
that little pinch of God goes right back
to God's great big loving heart.
That's how I reckon it's always been
and how it always will be."

I was eight, and I went away comforted,
knowing that my closest friend,
a dog called Don who'd been killed by a bus,
was now living happy and safe with God
who would feed him and take him for walks.

Now, understanding less than then,
but touching from time to time
that "pinch of God" in all things,
I give special thanks to my creator
for the friendship of animals in my life.

I can't count the times God has loved me
through small furred and feathered things,
how often I've been taught through them,
lessons of trust and playfulness,
simplicity and self-acceptance.

And since I do believe that heaven
is not so much a place as a state of being,
I can say to my own grandchildren,
"Yes, there are dogs in heaven."

 *Greenness*

Dear God, there are times
when I hear your voice most clearly
in greenness: in the singing of the sap,
the conversations of the leaves, the whisperings

of shoot and stem, root, sap and cell,
calling me back to creation
to feel again the freshness of you
running through everything
like a bright emerald current.

God of greenness, you know well my tendency
to fill my life with my own methods
of communication. Thank you
for constantly returning me
to the simplicity of yours.
Again I experience you in the rejoicing
of bare feet on a damp forest path,
in the wonder of the light thrown against
a kaleidoscope of tree ferns,
in the myriad textures of leaves,
the embrace of moss-clad trees,
in the shining of You beneath every surface.

Beloved Creator, coming to your greenness
is always a coming home,
a time of peace and grace
as the unimportant in me falls away
and I know again that bright green shoot
of my own beginning
which comes from you
and is one with you,
bright and beautiful God.

God of the Absurd

God of the absurd,
Creator of the feeding of pelicans,
the flight of the flamingo,
the departing of baboons,
the singing of peacocks,
and the hurrying of camels,
God of everything quaint, funny, incongruous,
you are the God who made me
and knows me through and through.

No one better than you
understands the contradictions
of my make-up, that mixture
of the sublime and the ridiculous
that is me. So, my loving Creator,
when I am experiencing the tension
of opposites, and am buried deep
in self-examination, please stop me
from taking myself too seriously.
Tune my ear to the laughter
of your universe,
and help me to understand it
as my own.

Roads

I enjoy looking at other people's roads.
They are different from mine
and yet basically the same.

They all facilitate journey
from here to there, self to other,
and they are all inter-connected.

The fact that I love my own road
with its comfortable landmarks
and familiar faces,
doesn't restrict my appreciation
of someone else's neighborhood.

And if I go into another area
and walk a mile or two with someone else,
I return as a larger being.
The love of my own road is deepened,
the appreciation of other roads is widened,
and I am blessed in the knowledge
that all roads lead to God.

*L*ove Your Enemy

I heard him say, Love your enemy.
And I thought, well, I did.
Sort of. From a distance.
As long as I don't have to talk to her
or share the same room for any time.
It wasn't that I hated her.
It was just a matter of principle.
I had to let her know
that I didn't approve.

But he kept saying, Love your enemy.
Over and over. Love your enemy.
And I thought, well, maybe
a bit closer wouldn't hurt.

A telephone call. Good morning.
Some questions of polite interest.
No need to compromise principles.
I could let her know
that I held no grudge.

He still kept saying it.
Love your enemy. Love your enemy.
So in the end, I had to go the whole hog.
Suddenly, there we were, talking about feelings,
laughing and crying and hugging each other.
And I was healed of the wound I'd given myself
with my judgmental attitudes.

So the next time he said, Love your enemy,
I knew clearly what he meant.
My real enemy
is self.
And I need all the love and forgiveness
I can get.

Teach Me to Love

Please God,
I would like to be a better lover.
Where I come from, the meaning
of that word is so distorted
that it's more about taking than giving
and I'm almost embarrassed to use it.
But to become a better lover is what I need
more than anything else.
I want to love with the spontaneity
of the small child, alive with delight
in love's perennial newness.
I want to love without discrimination,
hugging everything you have created,
earth, stars, lion, lamb, sunlight, shadows,
brothers and sisters, and especially
the stranger in myself.
I want to love recklessly
with the kind of commitment
which doesn't manufacture questions
or balance giving against getting,
but which takes a big step out
away from self-consciousness.
I want to love with trust.
There are fears in my life

which are born of ignorance
and which can only be erased
by love itself. I know, dear God,
that while selfishness is always with me,
love has a way of overcoming
the obstacles to its fulfillment.

So, please God, make me a better lover.
I make this prayer
in the name of the greatest lover
humanity has ever known,
Jesus, who stretched out his arms
to embrace the world and die for it.
Amen.

$\mathcal{D}$iscoveries Along the Road

My great and loving God,
I used to think of you as far away,
a God to travel to, to be attained
after a long life journey
through a difficult and hostile world.
Somehow, I'd got this idea
that if I stuck to the right path
with my eyes fixed on the road code,
at the end of it all, I'd arrive
somewhere close to your Kingdom.
A few times I did notice
that when I touched on a thought of you,
I felt a strange stirring within me
like a tiny first knocking on a door,
but that would pass and I'd plod on,
deeply afraid of getting lost.

Then came the day of the earthquake,
an upheaval which brought me to the ground
and had me calling out, like Job, for death.
Everything in my life was disaster.
But when at last, I could pick myself up,
I discovered an extraordinary thing.
The walls round my heart had fallen down,
revealing you at the core of my being.
God, you'd been with me all the time
and I hadn't known it!
What a breakthrough! What rejoicing!
I put the map in my pocket and danced.
Was there any discovery left in this life?

Indeed, there was.
The long months of weeping had cleared my eyes,
and as I journeyed on, I saw you,
brighter than day, in everything.
Not only were you at the heart
of every pilgrim on every road,
you were also a glowing light
in everything you had created–
each lamb and hawk, each rose and weed–
you yourself made a unity of your world,
weaving all things into a oneness of light.
Everything I saw as contained in you.
Surely this was the ultimate celebration!

But there was more to discover.
You, my loving God,
opened another door and showed me–
you were also the earthquake.

ision

Two people watched the same sunset.
One said: "At times like this I am afraid.
The sky is so vast, the sea so immense.
In comparison, I'm a speck of dust,
here today, gone tomorrow.
When I look at the hugeness of creation,
I feel my insignificance
and I wonder what my life
is all about."

The second person said:
"What a glorious sunset!
Just think!
I am the reason that this exists.
I am the only proof I have
of all the beauty in this world.
Without the gift of my life,
the gift of my senses,
all this would be as nothing.
I praise God that the universe is held
in the wonder of my being!"

The Woman of Samaria

I know a woman of Samaria
(Samaria is everywhere these days)
who went daily to draw water from the well,
and who heard that Jesus was coming
to the well on a certain day,
especially to see her.

The woman sent him a message:
"Master, this is a very great honor!

I'm overwhelmed by your kindness!
This well is a very busy place
but I shall be here all day
with a banquet prepared in you honor."

When the morning arrived, she was ready,
and, as usual, the place was busy.
Over 300 people came to the well that day.
Some looked at her banquet hungrily,
but she chased them away
and kept watch for her special visitor.

He didn't arrive.
There was no sign of him all day.

Disappointed, and a little angry,
she sent him another message:
"Master, what happened to you?
You said that you were coming to visit me
at the well."

Jesus sent a message back to her:
"I did. I was there more than 300 times."

The woman thought deeply on this,
then wrote to him again:
"Dear Jesus, please, in the future,
when you come to see me,
will you tell me who you are?"

I don't think she got an answer
to that one.

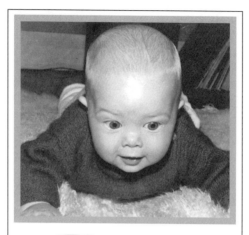

$\mathcal{T}$he Little Child

Dear God,
I would like to become a little child and rest
my soul in you.
I'm tired of the loneliness, tired of the struggle,
I want to surrender but I don't know how.
You see, I have this problem of being adult.
I belong to the generation which makes

decisions, plans, works, accepts
responsibility, takes pride in being independent.
Adults are supposed to manage their lives.
They are concerned with owning things and
making things happen, and they don't like to
look small or foolish.
Dear God, for a long time I've been living at
the center of a world which has prevented me
from entering the Kingdom of Heaven.

Father God, Mother God,
show me how to become your child.
I am aware of the advice that Jesus gives.
He does not say that we should remain in infancy.
He says that we should become as little children.
This tells me that I need to know the futility of
independence before I can let go of it.
It is the letting go which is difficult.
I know you are there, waiting to give yourself
to me, but I'm afraid to commit myself.
Please help me to loosen this grip on my pride
so that I can hold out my arms to you
and be enfolded in your love.

Praise

I've been looking for a suitable word
to praise you, Lord. Something enthusiastic
but not too formal, the sort of happy shout
a child gives to its mother.
I've tried Hallelujahs, Glorias, and Hosannas,
but really, what I'd like is a word
from my own language, a word that is me.
If I were a bellbird, I'd fill my throat
with ecstatic song. Or, as a lamb,
I could fling myself into spring dance.
As a mountain stream I would spill out
inarticulate babblings of joy.
And if I were the sea, my waves would explode
in a thunder of love for you.
Lord, you overwhelm me with your great good-
ness.
Praise should not be difficult and yet
I can't find the exact word. Perhaps
it doesn't exist, though if it does,
I'm sure that it sounds like "Yippee!"

The Bridge

There are times in life
when we are called to be bridges,
not a great monument spanning a distance
and carrying loads of heavy traffic,
but a simple bridge to help one person
from here to there
over some difficulty
such as pain, grief, fear, loneliness,
a bridge which opens the way
for ongoing journey.

When I become a bridge for another,
I bring upon myself a blessing,
for I escape from the small prison of self
and exist for a wider world,
breaking out to be a larger being
who can enter into another's pain
and rejoice in another's triumph.

I know of only one greater blessing
in this life, and that is,
to allow someone else
to be a bridge for me.

Currency of Living

I am not sure where I am with money.
When I've had very little of it,
I've been full of theories about sharing;
but when I've had more than enough,
the money changer in my temple
tends to label the surplus "my" and "mine."

I can't imagine the world without money
and yet it's difficult to use it wisely.
Jesus said that where our treasure is,
that's where our hearts are also.
I think I know what he meant,
but it still doesn't prevent me
from getting my values mixed up.
Where is my treasure?
Where is my heart?

I think that it helps when I remember
just whose this earth really is.
It's a truth that everything I have,
including myself, is a gift from God.
Nothing can be earned, nothing owned,
nothing labeled with my name.

When I remember that,
my heart shifts focus.
I lose sight of the "my" and "mine"
of material possessions
and I reach out to worship
not the gifts but the Giver.

Just Suppose

Suppose we're not a fallen people at all,
but a people on the way up;
not caterpillars that once were butterflies,
but actually the other way round.

Just suppose we have this wonderful God
who is so much in love with us,
He has drawn us out of the animal kingdom,
giving us the divine spark of His love
to grow into a fire within us and eventually
bring us to oneness with Him.

Just suppose we have this wonderful God
so totally, crazily in love with us,
first becomes one with His beloved,
taking on a human likeness
to join us in our growing pains,
suffering everything we might suffer,
to show us the truth of the empty chrysalis.

And just suppose that our words of fear
like disobedience and judgment and condemnation,
belong not to a God who is total Love
but to a half-grown people
trying to explain their incompleteness.

Suppose that the only ultimate truth
is that God is the source
and destiny of every soul.
Suppose that everything we are,
all our light and shade, our sin and celebration,
belongs wholly in God's love.
Suppose no one is ever lost to that love.

Wouldn't that be Good News?

A Wedding Song

In the beginning was Love.
Before the birth of the universe,
before the eruption of energy
that was to become matter,
there was Love.
And Love was God
and God was Love.

But to be true to Itself,
Love cannot exist
unless It is given away.
So Love breathed on the universe
and this earth was formed,
a planet of beauty,
a place of life and growth,
a nursery of Love.
And Love, being the Creator,
made all things of Itself
and in Its own image.

And Love looked upon Its creation
and saw one creature most lovely,
one creature whom It desired
above all others, to be Its own.

Love said: "This is my Beloved,
the one I choose to take to Myself,
and I will give birth to Myself
through this creature
and together we will fashion
an eternity of loving."

But here Love met with a difficulty,
for Love by Its very nature
cannot command, cannot dictate,
cannot impose Itself by force.
The creature had to be free to choose.
Love said: "I am Spirit. I am Truth.
My Beloved is bound by space and time
in a different dimension.
How can I reveal myself?
How can I help my Beloved
to be aware of me?"

Love had a plan.
It divided the creature in half
and set the halves apart on the earth.
The halves knew they were incomplete.
They were restless.
They roamed the earth,
looking for each other,
and when they found each other,
they sought to become one again.
In becoming one,
they discovered the wholeness of Love
within themselves
and in giving birth to themselves,
they gave birth to Love.

*F*amily Hymn

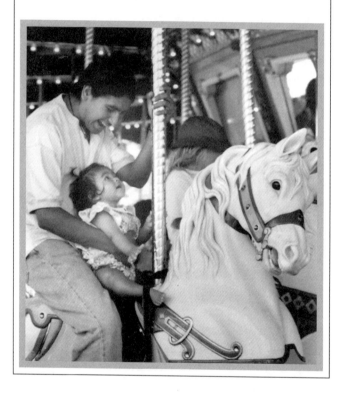

While the Angelus breaks the evening air
and prayers wash through cloisters,
Christ makes waves in his bath
and wants to know
if tiger sharks have fur.

While the scholar sits in awe
over an ancient manuscript,
tracking the history of his faith,
Christ nestles against her mother
and tells from a book held upside down,
a story about some clowns
who make rainbows out of ice cream.

While the priest at his desk,
somewhere between the front door
and the telephone,
writes another homily on love
and wonders if someone remembered
to repair the lectern microphone,
Christ comes sleepily and a little tearful
into his parents' bed
and says, as he plants cold feet
on his father's back,
"I love you a big much, Daddy."

While pilgrims journey
from shrine to shrine
on a long and well-blessed path,
Christ, laughing, takes her parents' hands
and shows them the shortcut to holiness.

The Way of Growth

I used to think that Advent and Easter
were separate events belonging to history
and certain times of the year,
but they are happening every day, every moment,
angels bright as air, chiming:
"He is born!" "He is risen!"
over every budding branch, each fist of fern,
making sense of the cycle of beginnings
and endings and beginnings in our lives.

The stories of earth which Jesus loved
go on proclaiming his truth for me,
reminding me that death and birth
precede each other on the path of growth.
For something to be born,
something else must die.
The placenta loses life
when a woman gives birth to a child;
the sunset is extinguished for a sunrise;
and my earlier images of Christ
must be crucified in me
so that he can fill me
with greater presence now.

Jesus Christ, Love of God,
thank you for your daily Advent
and Eastering in my life.
I hold my heart out wide
to embrace the deep mystery of your birth
and rebirth in me
and I ask for strength to accept
all the dyings in between.

A Friend in Need

Lord, I am hurting.
I feel like a tree
with its roots laid bare.
Suddenly there seems to be no support
and I don't know what to do about it.

I know that adversity builds character,
but that's tomorrow's story
and it has no meaning for now.
What I need, Lord, is a friend.

Choose my friend carefully.
Please, no one who's going to tell me
how to put my life straight,
no amateur analyst or teacher,
no preacher, no well-meaning person
who is going to "should" all over me.

I want someone to come in the door
with a smile and a big warm hug
to let me know I'm valuable
just as I am.
There'll be no advice,
no expectation of change.
My friend will already know
that pain is important in journey
and must be traveled through.

My friend will stay beside me
and hold my hand
while I make my own discoveries.

And then, when all this is over,
Lord help me to remember two things:
to say "Thank you,"
and to be a friend
with a big warm hug
to someone else in pain.

Seeing

Dear God,
I need to see myself
as you see me.
My own vision is fragmented.
I try to divide up my life
and reject those parts of me
I consider to be weak.
I waste time and energy
in the battle of self against self
and Lord, I always end up the loser.

Dear God,
help me to see myself
as you see me.
I forget that you made me just as I am
and that you delight in your creation.
You do not ask me to be strong;
you simply ask me to be yours.
You do not expect me to reject my weakness,
merely to surrender it to your healing touch.

Dear God,
when I can see myself
as you see me,
then I will understand
that this frail, tender, fearful, aching, singing,
half-empty, shining, shadowed person
is a whole being made especially by you
for your love.

 The Quiet Pool

There is within each of us
a quiet clear pool of living water
fed by one deep Source
and inseparable from it,
but so often hidden
by a tangle of activity
that we may not know
of its existence.

We can spend the proverbial forty years
wandering in strange deserts,
sinking unrewarding wells,
and moving on, driven by our own thirst,
but when we stop still long enough
to look inside ourselves, really look
beyond our ideas about water
and what and where it should be,
we discover it was with us all the time,
that quiet clear pool which is ageless,
the meaning of our existence
and the answer to all wanderings.

And as we drink,
we know what Jesus meant when he said
we'd never be thirsty again.

$\mathcal{T}$he Human Race

Who was it who said
that competition was a good idea?
Who reckoned it was important
to be first, best, biggest, richest,
fastest, brightest, top of the class?
Not Jesus, that's for sure.
Oh, he had his chance in the desert.
All the temptations given him
were a push for self-promotion.
He turned them down flat.
He knew that the secret of happiness
lay in making others happy,
in cooperation rather than competition,
in helping another unwrap her gift,
in listening to a brother's song.

Pursuit of excellence is part of growth
and important in our lives,
but that has got nothing to do
with standing on others
to increase our stature,
or leaving others behind
in order to get out front.
Isn't it better to share the pleasures
of all those around us
than to be restricted
to a small world of one?

Because that's the trouble with winning:
it leaves us standing on our own.
In fact, winning can be so lonely,
that often it feels like losing.

Prayer

"Don't call me, God. I'll call you."
Well, I don't mean it to be that way.
It's just that prayer tends to be on my terms,
when I've got the time and inclination,
and even then, I do all the talking,
as though God didn't already know
what was in my heart.

Yes, I'm aware that conversation
is a two-way business
but I guess it's easier for me to talk
because I've got a bit of a hearing problem,
and God's voice is so terribly quiet
that listening can be hard work.
It means tuning into a huge silence
in order to pick up a whisper or two.

I'm not good with silences.
They make me feel disconnected.
I want to shout down the line:
"Are you working? Is anybody there?"

I think I need some practice,
still times to sit with silence
and feel comfortable in it
so that I recognize the voice when it comes.

And who knows? Maybe one day I'll discover
that the best part of prayer
is to let God do most of the talking.

Childlike Trust

Whenever I look into
the clear eyes of children,
I feel a leap of light inside me
and with it, the touch of something new,
something green, something singing.

All of the child that was lost in me
is suddenly rediscovered,
and I know that I'm encountering
the freshness of God.

I think of how much Jesus needed
the company of children.
With adults' judgments round him,
a weight of shouldn't, mustn't, don't, can't,
continuously dumped on him
by insecure men and women,
how refreshing it must have been
for him to gather small children
close to his heart and so reinforce
his own clear vision
of the simplicity of Abba.

I think of his words as he blessed them:
"This is what heaven is all about."

To Mary

Mary, Mother of God,
you are the woman who is always there.

You celebrate with us
the Bethlehems and Nazareths
of our daily family living.
You stand by us in our Calvarys
and are with us at Pentecost.

Whatever our need
or wherever we are,
Mother of all seasons
you're there.

The images we have of you
will change with our life's journey.
You are the warmth of home and hearth.
You are the fertile full moon
embracing land and tide.
You are the little secret thing,
the oak seedling rooted in earth
and growing upward, outward,
to the Queendom of Heaven.
You are the Ark of the New Covenant.
You are the clay chalice
which holds the wine of Life,
the silent space of prayer in our lives.
You are the yes to God,
our yes to growth,
our yes to the birthing
of Christ in our world.

And however we see you
or fail to see you,
you are always there.

Music

This day of mine has been a very small tune, Lord,
enjoyable and sincere, but not well played.
The timing was wrong, I missed a few notes,
sorry about that, but never mind,
it was good to make music, your music, Lord,
and to listen to your songs through other people.

In this one small tune of a day,
there was a variety of moods:
slow rhythms for sadness or dreaming,
a lively bit of dancing here and there.
One time, some of the players came together
like an orchestra, with such full sound
that we forgot we'd ever played
in solo performance.
These are moments worth waiting for.

So I praise you, my wonderful composer God,
for the music of this one small day.
And I thank you for the way you've loved
harmony back into my mistakes,
even the big ones,
giving me the confidence to want to play
again tomorrow.

It's freedom to know that in your love,
the sweetest sounds are produced
by broken reeds.

Sacred Ground

We are standing on sacred ground.

Let our hearts take off their shoes
and come bare, trembling with awe,
into the Presence which burns too bright
and too close for ordinary vision.
Only a naked heart can see
that all round us, each clump of grass,
every leaf, twig, stone, and flower,
is a blazing torch, incandescent
with the one fire which has no name
except "I am."
And only a naked heart can know
that it too is a burning bush,
all of us caught in the one fire,
"we are" burning into "I am,"
brighter than a galaxy of suns.

Words cannot contain the moment;
but let's take it with us,
the feeling of awe and wonder.
Tomorrow's path might be dark,
difficult and sharp with stones,
but in this sacred place we feel
we may never wear shoes again.

The Bulldozer

God of journey,
your ways are not always gentle.
Sometimes you come into my life
like a bulldozer in top gear
and I, being so accustomed
to images of comfort and tender touch,
fail to recognize you.

As you tear away the support
I've carefully gathered round me,
ripping me wide open and moving me
in a direction I would not go,
I call you by the names of my fear–
Chaos, Darkness, Enemy, Evil–
and in my pain I cry out
to a tender image of you
for deliverance.

It is only later
when my wounds have healed
and I see how my life's been transformed,
how it has opened out
and been made rich with new growth,
only then do I glimpse the oneness
of the great Creator God
and I thank you with the names of praise–
Wisdom, Light, Friend, Goodness–
as I begin to understand
the true workings of Love.

Effort

Dear God,
I've just about busted a gut
trying to please you,
and if you really want to know,
I don't think I've got much of a response.

What's that you say?
I don't have to please you?
Why not?

Oh. Because I'm exactly as you made me
and you couldn't be more pleased with me
than you already are.
Well, if that's so, what's this effort about?
Why are people always telling me
to work for God, give to God,
live for God, etcetera.

I don't understand.
You say I do it not for you
but for myself. Oh, come off it, God.
I'd much rather be sitting back
in the sun, taking life easy.

Life is meant to be difficult, you say.
What on earth do you mean by that?
Sure, I'm looking round me.
What do I see?

The chicken struggling to hatch.
The plant struggling to grow.
As St. Paul says, the whole of creation
groaning in a struggle for birth.

I get it! A birth struggle!
You're telling me that effort is necessary for growth
and a part of the birthing process.
And I suppose you'll tell me my birth
is what I've been calling death.

Well God, if you don't mind my saying so,
from the way I feel now,
I reckon I'm almost there!

Fences

It is a strange truth in my life
that I spend more time looking at fences
than at wide open spaces.
If there's some barrier on the perimeter
you can be sure that I'll be there,
fussing and fretting about restrictions
and ignoring all the territory
which has been given to me.

It's as well I've got a God
who has a great sense of humor
because I'm a very slow learner,
wasting energy on the impossible
and neglecting what is mine.
You'd think I would know by now
that God's rules for creation
are very simple.
If a fence is insurmountable,
it's there because I need it.
The fence itself will never disappear
but when I have sufficiently grown,
I'll be able to step right over it
and it will be no barrier at all.

I Fly!

You big, bright, beautiful God,
this is my day for flying!
I reach out to the bigness of you.
I touch the brightness of you
and I feel the beauty of you
in the center of my living.
Today you bear me up, up,
past my doubts about both of us,
to the certainty of your love.

Today, God, I know you.
All those words I learned
are burnt up in your fire.
You are sun to my Icarus,
candle to my moth.
Today I fly
and am dissolved in you!

And if tomorrow I am grounded
by a weight of anxieties,
if my feet are heavy and there are clouds
between me and the sun,
then let me keep hold
of the warm place in my heart
reminding me that today I flew
and was kissed by God.

The Search

Beloved,
all day I searched for you,
pursuing your image in mountains,
rivers, caves, and clouds,
seeing but not seeing you
in wild and windswept places,
on open roads and deep city streets.
Beloved, I listened for your voice
in falling rain and the sound of birds,
hearing, yet not hearing you in children's laughter.
I followed your footprints through a desert.
I called you by all the names of love I knew.
Recklessly, I squandered my heart

for a glimpse of you in a familiar face;
but even there you remained hidden.

Beloved, all day I sought you,
and you eluded me.
In my hunger I sifted through my prayers,
pressing words and phrases on my tongue
for some taste of your presence.
Where were you?

By the close of day I had not found you.
I'd traveled to the edge of expectation
and was tired.
My voice was stilled, my hunger self-consumed.
In that hour of calm between light and dark,
I entered a silence and rested.
And you came to me!
You!
Lovelier than loveliness,
finer than fine,
you came with the suddenness of light
and the swiftness of laughter,
surprising me to tears
with the sound of my name.
(Why did I think you had left me?)

Then gently you led me to the garden
and we walked in the cool of the evening
as we did those other times.

The Heart of Stone

There are times when I've cried out,
"God, give me back my heart of stone
and a ladder so that I can climb
up to my head and live there
with doors and windows shut on feeling.
God, God, I'm tired of all the hurt.
For a little while, let me live
a second-hand life. Let me tread
the safe path of other people's ideas.
Just let me drop this awesome responsibility
you have given me, to grow
through love and pain."

Then I remember what it's like
to exist with a heart of stone.
How cold and dead I felt inside,
and how divided the world was
when viewed without love in my heart.

Remembering, I pour myself before God
and whisper into His waiting,
"My God, there is no going back.
It has to be a soft heart,
one that is always vulnerable
to the love and wounding
which is life,
which is growth,
which is You."

Keep within me, my God,
the heart of flesh.

The Time of Quiet

Sometimes, on a still morning,
it seems that all the earth
is breathless with love
for the God it conceals and reveals.
The brown stones at the water's edge
are set like some ancient language

pronouncing the truth of God
where our words fail us,
and the sea, the hills, the early mist,
become like watercolor painting
on a fine gauze curtain
drawn over a tabernacle.
At such times we feel so close
to the eternal light
which lies behind everything,
that we can almost reach out and touch.
God wraps us up in the quiet
of Christ, and invades us,
making us captive to a love too deep
for naming in this world.
All we know in this perfect moment
is that we too, can walk on water.

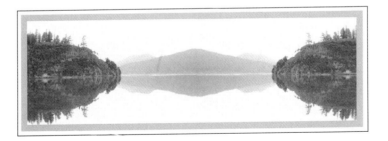

*H*ead *and Heart*

Head said: "I contain the law."
Heart said: "I am full of feeling."

Head said: "I am logic. I am structure.
I am the stake which supports the young plant."
Heart said: "I am love. I am mystery.
I am the creative force of life."

Then Head and Heart began to quarrel.
Head said: "You are emotional and irrational.
You live in a world of chaos."
Heart replied: "You are cold and unfeeling.
You do not live at all."
So Head and Heart went to God
and asked if they could be separated.

God laughed at them and said:
"Not even God can do that.
You two belong to each other.

Apart, I'm afraid you're nothing.
Head, you are the container.
Heart, you are the contents.
The container without the contents
is as hollow as a drum,
all noise and no substance.
The contents without the container
will disperse and be wasted,
good for nothing at all.
There's no way you can be separate
and lead useful lives.

Head and Heart grew anxious.
"But we are so different.
How can we find peace?"

God said: "Draw close and become lovers.
Respect each other. Nurture each other.
Help each other to be equal.
You will come together as one,
and when you are one,
a truly amazing thing will happen."

Head and Heart sat up at that.
"What kind of thing?" they asked.

But God only smiled
and said: "Wait and see."

The Harvest

You came down the corridor of afternoons
to the hour of our toil in the vineyard.
We were so concerned with the task before us,
we did not see that the sun had tipped sideways
in homage, or that the wind in the leaves
was stilled. You were a stranger there,
willing to help, another shoulder for the baskets,
extra hands to gather the hanging fruit.
If your palms seemed darkly bruised,
then so did ours, for the grapes were over-ripe
and juice stained our skin.
But as you worked with us,
we did observe a quickening, a strength in our bones
as though we had rested for a night.
We laughed and talked and gave you instruction
in the art of making wine. We showed you the vats
where the grapes were crushed underfoot, pressed
to fill the dark stone cellars on the hill.
The wine of the region was famous, we said,
and was shipped all over the world.

As shadows lengthened, our day, it seemed,
grew younger.
We washed at the stream, then walked the long road
to the village, arm in arm, singing like children
and falling against each other with laughter.
Only when you had gone, did we ask questions.
How was it that already, we felt full of new wine?

_D_rought

He came to me for water
and my well was empty.
I said, "It's not my fault.
It seems that everyone
is thirsty, and I'm only me,
one small well. When I'm down
to the last drop, that's it.

What do you expect? Miracles?
I'm sorry, but that's your department."

He laughed. He usually does
when I get mad about something.
"Everything is miracle," he said.
"Can you name me one thing which isn't?
The greatest miracle here
is that you're not only you.
One small well, yes, but connected
to a great underground river
which will never run dry.
Know where the water comes from
and take time to fill.
It's as simple as that."

I said, "Well, of course I knew that,
but I was so busy, I forgot."

He smiled, "Some time you must meet
my friends Mary and Martha.
You remind me a lot of them."

"Which one?" I asked.

"Both," he replied.

The Call

J esus says, "Come, follow me."
I say,
"Lord, you're calling the wrong person.
I'm not the following type.
It takes me all my time
to stand on my own two feet."

And he says, "I love you."

I say,
"Now, don't get me wrong, Lord.
I do all I can within reason,
but I can't afford to go overboard.
I mean, I have to live in this world."

And he says, "I love you."

I say,
"It's all very well to talk about love,
but love is dangerous.

It can get people crucified.
At the best it can be misunderstood.
If I go round telling people I love them,
someone's going to lock me up."

And he says, "I love you."

I say,
"The trouble is, I'm not ready.
Come back in a few years
when I've got my life sorted out.
By then I should have something
to offer you."

And he says, "I love you."

I say,
"Lord, don't look at me like that.
You're making it very difficult.
All right, I'll spell it out.
I'm a sinner. I'd let you down.
I'd give my life to you
and then try to take it back again.
I'm weak, Lord."

And he says, "I love you."

I say,
"You don't understand what I'm telling
you.
I'd deny you and betray you.
There'd be times when I'd crucify you.
And what would you think of me then?"

And he says,
"I love you."

alm Sunday

No donkey this time
but a borrowed Honda 550.
Jesus is riding into town
with a black leather jacket,
jeans frayed at the knees,
and L-O-V-E tattooed
on the knuckles of his right hand.
Those who saw him
said his smile was like the sun,
warming shadowed corners
and causing the way to blossom
unexpectedly.
Those who saw him told
of all the light left over
to be taken home and set
in eyes, in hearts,
and at windows for strangers.
It was like a miracle,
they said.

The rest of us missed it.
We were in another part of the city,
waiting for the Messiah.

Mandatum

Jesus, I would like you to wash my feet.
I've come a long distance to ask you this,
although I've frequently gone
from my house to yours
with my boxes of fragrant ointments
and my tears,
sincerely believing that this
was the best I could offer you,
that it was my love which mattered.

I was eager,
but I didn't know much about discipleship
or the true nature of love;
and you, always gentle,
never told me I was wrong,
but patiently waited
for me to grow in understanding.

It has taken a long time, Lord,
but now I fling open the door to my
house
and invite you in to cleanse my feet
of the dust of my many wanderings.
I will not feel shame to have you kneel
before me,
but I will gladly receive the mastery of
your love;
for in receiving I learn the truth of giving
and I become your servant in being
served.

Lord Jesus, please,
I would like you to wash my feet.

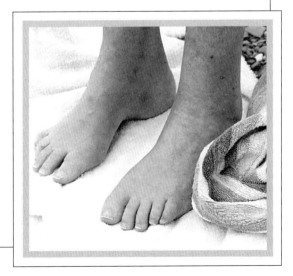

Kenosis

Jesus, dear brother,
how well you knew
the seasons in your life.
God planted in flesh,
you grew and flowered for thirty years
for three years of seeding
and that final emptying
of yourself.

Jesus, I need your sense of timing.
I am so keen to grow
that I want all seasons at once,
to flower, bear fruit, die to self,
before self is fully grown.

I know that only the mature plant
can come into fruiting
and yet here I am,
reaching out for tomorrow,
ignoring the small plant
which needs nurturing,
which constantly cries out:
"What about me?"

Gift me, Jesus, with the wisdom
of those thirty years
of growing and waiting

and show me the importance
of loving myself.
I need to know that the hungry ego
is not an enemy to be destroyed.
It is a manifestation
of my need for growth.

I must draw life into myself
and mature to the fullness
God has planned for me.
When my time is come,
my ego will split wide open
like the ripened seedpod
it should be
and empty itself
for others.

Grief

For most of us,
death appears as a fixed horizon
and those who pass over it
leave an emptiness we must fill
with a season of grieving.
And yet, with our sorrow
there is also a knowledge of light,
a certainty that the sense of loss
belongs not to any ending
but to the limitation of our vision.
Death is an experience for those left behind,
not for those who are moving
from one stage of living to another.

It is the Christ who dwells within us
who is free to step back and forth
over the horizon of death,
containing our grief in His Passion
and our knowledge of light
in his transcendence,
showing us that death and resurrection
are the two sides of the one coin.

So while grief goes on, the tears, the hurting,
I know in the truth of Jesus Christ
that the hollowness I feel
at the departure of loved ones,
is in reality, the hollowness
of the empty tomb.

Release

It was a bit like
the opening of a tomb, really,
the lid of the cage pulled back
and quick bright life spilling out
with an eagerness to fly.

As I watched the wingbeat
of those pigeons, I felt murmurings
against the bars of my heart.

All the love imprisoned within me
fluttered for release. Blessings unspoken,
smiles concealed, acts of kindness
which had never got off the drawing board,
clamored for the light of day.

I wondered about the cost
of opening the cage
and letting love spread its wings.
I felt a bit frightened.
When I'd given everything away,
could I live with an empty heart?

What I'd forgotten, of course,
was the homing instinct of love,
and how, unlike pigeons,
love always returns
with more than it takes away.
The other thing I forgot
was how love enlarges the heart
to take its increase,
multiplying and enlarging,
multiplying and enlarging,
until the little cage
is as big as the Kingdom of Heaven.

$\mathcal{S}$pringtime Jesus

You, Springtime Jesus,
just as I'd settled down for winter,
you broke into my heart
and danced your love right across it
in a mad excess of giving.
Just as I'd got comfortable
with bare branches and unfeeling,
just as my world was neatly black and white,
there you were,
kicking up flowers
all over the place.
Springtime Jesus,
I tried to find a way to tell you
that there were places
where you could and could not dance.
I wanted to guide you on my paths
and have you sign the visitors' book;
but you laughed right through my words
and sang to me your melting song,
causing sap to fire the branches,
causing the flames of buds
to flicker into green bonfires,
causing a windquake of blossom,
causing burstings, searings, breakings,
causing growth-pain,
causing life.

Springtime Jesus,
the fullness of life can be frightening
and I'm lacking in courage.
It isn't easy to live with a heart
that's wide open to invasion.
Teach me, Jesus, how to move with you,
step for step, in your love dance.
Touch my fears with your melting song.
Gift me with your laughter,
and, in the mystery of your Springtime,
show me the truth of the blossoming Cross.

Loaves and Fishes

The feeding of the five thousand
is a little different these days,
with loaves and fishes changed in appearance.

But I believe that people are much the same,
and Christ's presence among us is still miracle
whether we recognize him or not.

For the wonder of Jesus is
that he always oversteps the narrowness
of the expectations we place upon him.
He turns up out of place and time
to bless and bless and bless yet again,
without leaving so much as a business card
or an advertisement for the local church.
But we know something has happened.
There is a transformation
in the sharing of food and lives,
in the laughter of children,
in the special mood which hangs over us,
unnamed and yet fragrant with love.
Some of us know who is present.
We look for him in the crowd, asking,
"Excuse me, are you the Christ? Is it you?
Or you? Are you the one?"
Gradually there is an awakening
to the truth of the loaves and fishes miracle.
Christ has so multiplied Himself among us,
that he has made us all into Himself,
and we are all sacrament to each other.

Your Psalm

(This space is reserved for your own prayer written from the gospel of your life.)